FUNNIEST EVERTON QUOTES... EVER!

Also available

THE FUNNIEST EVERTON QUOTES... EVER!

by Gordon Law

Printed in Europe and the USA.
ISBN: 9781696969956
Imprint: Independently published

Photos courtesy of: Jaroslav Moravcik/Shutterstock.com; mooinblack/Shutterstock.com

Contents

Introduction

Dixie Dean is regarded as the finest player to pull on an Everton shirt – and is arguably the greatest English striker ever.

He not only helped the Toffees to an FA Cup and two First Division titles in their golden era, but he had a sense of humour that matched his incredible scoring record which included 60 goals in one season.

"People ask me if that 60-goal record will ever be beaten," he said. "I think it will. But there's only one man who'll do it. That's that fella who walks on the water. I think he's about the only one."

And he loved nothing better than winding up local rivals Liverpool: "I just used to turn round to the crowd and bow three times to them."

Fellow legend Brian Labone also loved to fire shots at the Reds, famously saying: "One Evertonian is worth 20 Liverpudlians."

The Scouse wit of Joe Royle has provided many laughs, as have the strange musings of fellow manager Roberto Martinez or the rants at referees by David Moyes.

There have been bonkers remarks from Neville Southall, weird sound bites from Mike Lyons, comic one-liners from Wayne Rooney, while Bill Kenwright has shown his humorous side.

Many of their brilliant bloopers can be found in this unique collection of funny Everton quips and I hope you laugh as much reading this book as I did in compiling it.

Gordon Law

THE FUNNIEST EVERTON QUOTES... EVER!

A FUNNY
OLD GAME

"I've never been so certain about anything in my life. I want to be a coach. Or a manager. I'm not sure which."

Phil Neville

"The football played by Big Sam was awful, if it could even be called football."

Nikola Vlasic slams former manager Sam Allardyce

"Have boots won't travel, that's me."

Gordon West on not flying out with England's 1970 World Cup squad

"I never went into a game frightened of anybody. I always thought I could handle most of them and sort them out if need be."

Andy Gray

"It's a lot easier to rip the picture up than to paint it. I've spent my career ripping the picture up. I can kick the ball high into the stand and people say, 'Oh, great defending'."

Richard Gough

"I discovered it's not the gloves but what's in them that counts."

A light-bulb moment for Neville Southall

"When there are just 500 fans inside a ground, you can hear everything they say, every little word. So that's what turns you from a kid into a man."

How Jordan Pickford became an adult

"I didn't bother to take them normally because I didn't consider them to be a real goal."

Bob Latchford on penalties

"You get your 15 minutes of fame, I hear, and I've had 14. The clock's ticking."

Tim Howard can't wait to quit football

"People ask me if that 60-goal record will ever be beaten. I think it will. But there's only one man who'll do it. That's that fella who walks on the water. I think he's about the only one."
Dixie Dean

"It's as if someone controls him from the stands, like a video game. I have never seen a human run with the ball at that speed."
Mikel Arteta on Lionel Messi

"It's a bullet I must bite every year."
John Heitinga is biting with anger at a lack of game time

"I would go into the dressing-room beforehand and disco music would be blaring out, the kit men were booting tennis balls around and my teammates would be wolfing down three bananas each minutes before kick-off."

Marco Materazzi on 'bad' pre-match rituals

"When my agent told me I could sign for Everton I was like, 'Thank you God'."

Royston Drenthe praises the Lord

"I feel I have been cryogenically frozen for a year, but once I'm defrosted I'll be alright again."

Gareth Farrelly looking for a recall

"I am used to playing for a coach and supporters who prefer that you play yourselves out of trouble at the back and pass to a teammate. At Everton it was more to do with kicking the ball as far from your goal as possible."

Per Kroldrup has fond memories

"We now have a manager who wants to win games."

Kevin Sheedy takes a swipe at David Moyes after Roberto Martinez joins

"People have said it's psychological, but in my head I know that's not true."

Louis Saha

"If there were no such thing as football, we'd all be frustrated footballers."

Mike Lyons

"I spent four indifferent years at Goodison Park, but they were great years."

Martin Hodge – so which was it?

"It couldn't have been any better if it had been Cindy Crawford on the other end asking me out for dinner."

John Spencer after receiving a call that confirmed a problematic transfer to Motherwell was back on

"After that incredible first goal [for Everton] against Arsenal, when Arsene Wenger was talking to the world's media about his special talent, Wayne was already out on his BMX bike, meeting his mates outside the local chip shop. He even ended up kicking a ball against the wall with them."

Wayne Rooney's agent Paul Stretford

Reporter: "The [Prague] pitch looks good?"
Lee Carsley: "Yeah, no bobbles... but I'll find one."

The Everton star isn't confident about his first touch ahead of Ireland's game against the Czechs

"Look at the players who came from here and went to a big club – Rodwell, Fellaini, Rooney. Good players have stayed here a year, maybe two or three, and gone on to a big team. Hopefully it will be the same for me."

Romelu Lukaku is already planning his exit after joining the Toffees

"When I put my shirt on I gave everything. I've got the scars to prove it – too many really."

Duncan Ferguson

"On a scale of one to 10, how happy am I? Try 12."

Andy Johnson after signing from Palace

"A huge bulk filled the doorway and I realised it was the great Dixie Dean. 'Hello, Dixie', I whispered. 'Hello kid, don't call me Dixie. Call me Bill'."

Gordon Watson was put in his place when meeting the Everton great

"I'm more afraid of my mum than Sven-Goran Eriksson or David Moyes."

Wayne Rooney

"I'm sure there has been a lot written about me but luckily enough I never read it!"

Duncan Ferguson didn't like speaking to the press or even buying newspapers

"If you don't believe you can win, there is no point in getting out of bed at the end of the day."
Neville Southall

"I don't accept not playing – I want to be playing – and I'm not learning to deal with it. I'm just dealing with it, if you like, because I don't want to ever learn how to deal with that."
Richard Wright on dealing with the English language

"Most footballers are grounded. You do come across the odd numpty."
Leighton Baines

"Harry Catterick is supposed to have called me the 'Last of the great Corinthians'. But to me he used to say, 'Brian, look on the bright side. If you'd have been a race horse, they'd have shot you'."

Brian Labone had a recurring Achilles injury problem

"Hand on heart, I never started anything, never once. That's the truth. I finished a few."

Duncan Ferguson. Wigan's Paul Scharner, who had a notable clash with Ferguson, once said: "I began to appreciate how he earned his reputation as a hard man. It was a nice punch, I have to say."

"I know it's 100 per cent the right decision but I'm going to sulk all day."

Phil Neville after Everton's game against Tottenham is postponed

"I don't think I could jump over a car now. At my age, I'm grateful to be able to jump in one."

Duncan McKenzie was known for leaping over Minis at training

"At the time, at 16, I remember looking around the Everton first team and knowing I was the best player."

Wayne Rooney

"It's not all bad being an Evertonian. Imagine if you supported Birmingham City, then you'd really have something to moan about."

Bob Latchford

"I hate the modern gloves. They are so big and thick, goalkeepers can't feel the ball. It's like trying to drive a car in boxing gloves."

Neville Southall

"I'd have broken every bone in my body for every club I played for, but I would have died for Everton."

Dave Hickson

"When he realised I was getting so much of the limelight, I felt he resented it."

Wayne Rooney on David Moyes in his book My Story

"I'd have gone almost anywhere just to get away from David Moyes. He appeared overbearing."

Rooney continues

"If you were to offer us fourth from bottom now we'd take it."

Kevin Campbell is aiming high ahead of Everton's 2004/5 season

"That midfield would have tackled a crisp packet if it had floated across the pitch!"
Duncan Ferguson on the 'Dogs of War' midfield

"I think it's fair to say we're an improving team and a team that's getting better."
Phil Neville

"I went on to play for other clubs, and although I always wanted to win, losing never really seemed to hurt anymore."
Kevin Ratcliffe

"I'd love to sign for Everton. They are offering me a wonderful four-year deal, I could earn three times as much as I do now at Anderlecht. I know Everton are not a top club, they don't play in Europe."

Tomasz Radzinski, honest as the day is long

"When I was younger I'd watch Everton, I followed them a lot."

Richarlison. Did you really?

"Some goalkeepers are really sexy with their feet. I have a little sexiness with my feet, but I don't like to bring it out."

Tim Howard

"It feels great [to be back]. To be honest, I've kept it quiet for the last 13 years, but I've actually been wearing Everton pyjamas at home with my kids. I had to keep that a bit quiet!"

Wayne Rooney on returning to the Toffees

"Look at boxers, you see them praying before a fight, and then they try to punch someone's head off. I am big and powerful, I use the attributes God has given me."

Victor Anichebe

"Fourth spot is what we're aiming for – we don't want to be second-best."

Phil Neville is not so sure

"When I heard that I thought, 'Jesus, does every manager in the Premier League think I'm this nutcase who drinks every night?'"

Don Hutchison on being rejected by Blackburn when he was at West Ham

Journalist: "How can Rob Green get over a mistake like that?"

Tim Howard: "A lot of alcohol."

The keeper on his opposite number who gifted the USA a goal at the 2010 World Cup

"It was God's will that I return to Everton."

Alex Nyarko reckons it's his time after two years away on loan

"When I scored my first goal for England, I was so excited I didn't know what to do or where to run. David [Beckham] just pointed and said, 'Well the England fans are that way, mate'."

Wayne Rooney gets a helping hand

"I was told to go out and kick him, which I did. For the rest of the game he was after me, but I was just laughing at him and winding him up."

Joe Parkinson versus Paul Ince in the 1995 FA Cup Final

"We played to our capabilities. That's what this team is capable of."

The very capable Phil Neville

"I think I've gained most of my strength from the beard."

Tim Howard after saving a penalty against Aston Villa

"Always nice to see a few familiar faces."

Wayne Rooney's jokey tweet, accompanied with a photo of him celebrating in front of angry Man City fans after scoring

"I told him he was a jammy b*stard and he thanked me for the goal!"

Phil Neville on what he said to Paul Scholes after scoring an own goal against United

"I discussed it with [Roberto Martinez], I spoke to Chelsea, I spoke to my mother, and eventually she said, 'Go to Everton'. I haven't regretted it."

Romelu Lukaku takes his mum's advice to sign for Everton

"I scored my first goal at Norwich and I did a daft 50-yard dash round the ground waving to the crowd and everybody was laughing so much that I've done it ever since."

Dave Watson

"One fan said, 'You old git!' – he's got a point you know."

Nigel Martyn, aged 38, after a win at Villa

"I'm trying to remember whose backside I had a bit of help from – there's a fair chance it was Jan Molby's, isn't there?"

Gary Stevens on netting his winner at Liverpool in 1987

"When I signed, I was told I was going to be the first of many big money signings. Someone was telling fibs."

John Collins after leaving Monaco to join Everton

"He blatantly stole results from us on more than one occasion."

Bob Latchford's view of referee Clive Thomas

"Not many people can say they scored at the Bernabeu so I was quite pleased, although I don't know how happy [keeper] Bobby Mimms was."

Alan Harper scored an own goal in a friendly against Real Madrid

"Exhausted? I had to go off with a heart attack."

Dave Watson, aged 38, on marking Arsenal's Nicolas Anelka

"Everyone will go away happy today, except us."

How about Aston Villa? Phil Neville after Everton's 3-2 loss against the Villans

CALL THE MANAGER

THE FUNNIEST EVERTON QUOTES... EVER!

"Being a big centre half myself, it was obviously me who taught him to go and just gently lift it over the goalkeeper!"
David Moyes takes the praise for Steven Pienaar's classy lob against Arsenal

"I don't think the contact was as severe as the player made out. That part of the pitch was uneven, but it won't need any rolling now."
Howard Kendall after Duncan Ferguson saw red for clashing with Paulo Wanchope

"He's like a human sling."
David Moyes after his side concede two Rory Delap-assisted goals from his throw

"There must have been a few clubs smiling at the irony of a Liverpool manager complaining about a referee at Anfield."

Joe Royle after a Merseyside derby

"Maybe I have a bit of responsibility by playing too much attacking-minded players and not as many defending-minded players. I should have got back to being a bit more boring and a bit less adventurous."

A sarcastic Sam Allardyce after a 4-0 defeat with no shots on target against Tottenham

"Blackpool are flying by the skin of their pants."

David Moyes

"It was a rubbish decision by the referee and he had a poor game all day."

David Moyes fumes at Jon Moss' decision to show Steven Pienaar a red card

"I'm told that David Ginola ran up the tunnel and dived in the bath."

Joe Royle

"Was it five? I was sure it was six. The radio guy said something about it being five, so I'm glad I didn't pick him up on it now!"

David Moyes loses count after the 5-1 thumping of Hull

"I wasn't aware. But if that was the case, maybe he will have to hit a woman in every game in order to score two goals. So I'll make sure that that happens in the finishing routine!"

Roberto Martinez jokes with the press after hearing Romelu Lukaku had accidentally fired a ball at a lady in the crowd during the warm-up. The striker ended up scoring a brace in the 3-0 victory

"The team Man City had could probably play in the NBA. They were like the New York Knicks."

David Moyes on Manchester's new basketball team

"Overall I thought his contribution to the game was very good. I thought he kicked well, commanded his box, was sharp out behind the defenders. But I've told him that he should have saved both goals."

David Moyes on Richard Wright's debut

"You can knock some of the passing that goes astray but you can't knock me for that, I don't pass the ball."

Sam Allardyce

"I've just seen the replay again for the first time."

David Moyes is caught in a time loop

"Maybe he got caught up in the whole day and thought he was going to get a medal as well."

David Moyes takes a swipe at referee Rob Styles' display in the game against Chelsea

"I wouldn't call it a crisis, it's just a fact that we find it hard to score at home."

Walter Smith after Everton's eighth goalless draw of the season out of 11

"I think there was just a little change today and I started to smell that things were improving a little bit."

David Moyes has a good nose for the game

"I had to say on Saturday that we didn't deserve the penalty, in the same breath today I have to say that we did."

David Moyes' super breathing powers after Everton's 1-1 draw against Blackburn

"In the end, if you can't mark them, foul them."

Sam Allardyce's mantra after Everton lose to champions-elect Manchester City

"The ref was a big-time homer, more interested in his rub-on suntan."

David Moyes on Jeff Winter

"I'm going to play at centre half against Aston Villa on Saturday."

David Moyes looking to save the day for his injured side

"I'm just glad the referees can't understand what he's saying to them."

Joe Royle on Duncan Ferguson

"We've given up on getting penalties. We don't even appeal anymore or jump up and down on the touchline."

David Moyes after Andy Johnson had yet another spot-kick denied

SEEING RED

"Everton have always been noted for going out on the pitch to play football. We got called the School of Science quite rightly. The other lot, the Reds, well they were a gang of butchers. They should have been working in an abattoir. McNab, McKinlay and the Wadsworths, God bless my soul, they'd kick an old woman."

Dixie Dean

"You always knew when it was derby week [on Merseyside]. The postman would say, 'We'll be ready for you'. Then the milkman would come round, 'You're in for it Saturday'. Then it would be the taxi driver. You never got away from it."

Gordon Lee

"Since Grobbelaar got done for bribery, I've sometimes thought he might have let it in, and it's been playing on my mind for years."

Alan Harper on scoring an unlikely goal against the Reds

"Don't forget boys, one Evertonian is worth 20 Liverpudlians."

Brian Labone

"I sit in this room and I know I am surrounded by Evertonians because you are all beautiful people. Kopites are all ugly b*stards aren't they?"

Gordon West

"When you score against that lot it's the best feeling in the world and anything goes."
Kevin Ratcliffe after netting a screamer at Liverpool in 1986

"I even tell a journalist that I still hate Liverpool and all hell breaks loose in the papers. There are headlines, 'Rooney: I Hate Kop'. But that feeling, that dislike, doesn't go away."
Wayne Rooney

"Most of my family still supports Liverpool, but a few switched allegiances to follow my career. I'm not sure if they thank me for it too often!"
Alan Harper

"I usually put one finger up signalling a goal, but it being the Kop end, two fingers just automatically went up. I got hauled up in front of the FA and I was like [3-2-1 game show host] Ted Rogers trying to go from two fingers to one and trying to convince them it wasn't a V-sign."

Kevin Sheedy

"There was nothing like quietening that Kop. When you stuck a goal in there it all went quiet, apart from a bit of choice language aimed in your direction! Scoring there was a delight to me. I just used to turn round to the crowd and bow three times to them."

Dixie Dean, the arch provocateur

"I didn't hit it off with the Liverpool coaches. They were a bit funny towards me. Perhaps it had something to do with wearing the Everton colours."

Wayne Rooney went to Melwood for a trial at the age of nine

"When I got goals against other clubs I was delighted, but when I scored against Liverpool I only had sympathy for them."

Dixie Dean

"No amount of money could make me play for Liverpool."

Tim Cahill

"I thought I would shut them up. Gordon, the miner's son and conker champion from Barnsley, was going to shut the Kop up! So I sauntered along, showed them my bum then blew some kisses. A year later, I got the handbag. It shut me up – it stuck with me the rest of my life."

Gordon West on getting a handbag thrown at him from the Kop end

"We've beaten them already this season so if we're a small club, I hope other small clubs beat them."

Lee Carsley after Rafa Benitez said following a 0-0 derby draw: "When you play against the smaller clubs at Anfield, you know the game will be narrow."

THE FUNNIEST EVERTON QUOTES... EVER!

CAN YOU MANAGE?

"People think Paul and I have a father-and-son relationship. Well, I've got two sons and I have never felt like hitting them, but I have certainly felt like smacking him."

Walter Smith on Paul Gascoigne

"I think he's Uranian."

Gordon Lee when asked about Imre Varadi's nationality

"He's only 25, albeit a Nigerian 25, and so if that is his age he's still got a good few years ahead of him."

David Moyes questions the age of his striker Yakubu

Howard Kendall: "How was Pat Van Den Hauwe on the flight?"

Journalist: "It was like guiding a rabid dog home."

The manager wanted to make sure his defender made it back from pre-season

"Landon [Donovan] said he had the flu. I told him people from Los Angeles don't get flu."

David Moyes

"Duncan Ferguson became a legend before he became a player."

Joe Royle

"If he likes to play football then he needs to leave Everton."

Ronald Koeman's not so subtle message to Oumar Niasse

"I hope he scores a hat-trick every week in the under-23s."

Koeman still won't recall Niasse to the first team

"Mickey [Thomas] gave you everything on the pitch, but there was no real discipline. He even managed to write off a club car in a car wash."

Howard Kendall

"Now is the time to fulfil your world-class potential."

Roberto Martinez to Gerard Deulofeu. Erm?

"I think you do not have a better English player."

Roberto Martinez on Tom Cleverley

"For me Gareth Barry is one of the best English players ever."

Roberto Martinez

"He was a good lad but mental."

Davie Moyes on Thomas Gravesen

THE FUNNIEST EVERTON QUOTES... EVER!

LIFESTYLE CHOICE

"Wayne's the antithesis of Beckham. He'll never wear a sarong out in Liverpool, for example."

Dave Barraclough, designer of Wayne Rooney's clothing brand

"The birth was always planned around football. I didn't want to miss any games."

Richard Wright after his wife had their baby induced so he could play in the Merseyside derby

"It's a dreadful town, a sh*t city. I try to avoid visiting the central parts of Liverpool."

Tobias Linderoth

"Nobody even recognised me when I went back and the commentators thought I was a new signing."

Paul Bracewell got an extreme haircut from his wife

"I was recognised too much [in Liverpool] and sometimes women would suddenly climb all over me."

Marouane Fellaini

"U women of [sic] always wanted equality until it comes to paying the bills #hypocrites."

Phil Neville tweets his sister Tracey

"I no longer drink. At most I will have a glass of wine... I want to play until I am 38 and I think Everton can win the title."

Paul Gascoigne – is he really off the booze?

"It was a big mistake of my wife. Put her under pressure!"

Ronald Koeman is criticised for having red decorations on his Christmas tree

"When I was playing, I couldn't afford a pair of boots, never mind boutiques."

Dixie Dean to George Best on the rising players' wages

"The story's true, but the stories with the girls –
they just give it, like, a little extra."

**Royston Drenthe admits he went to
Everton's training ground at 2am but
didn't confirm rumours he was intending
to use the club's hot tub with two women**

"I had two obsessions [as a child] – football
and Ninja Turtles... We copied [the Ninja
moves] off TV until we got them perfect, and if
anybody else wanted to be Raphael, I used to
sit on them until they gave in. I rated Raphael
up there alongside Alan Shearer."

Wayne Rooney

"We have to look after Wayne and that includes every Evertonian. If you see him out in the street, send him home. Sir Alex Ferguson used to offer £100 to anyone telling him where his young stars were. I might do the same."

David Moyes

"Never mix perms and drinking, it's a recipe for disaster."

Mick Lyons

"I prefer that people are now talking about me as a player rather than about my hair."

Marouane Fellaini

"I came home and said to my dad, 'Are we Irish?'. He replied, 'How do I know?'."
Wayne Rooney

"Phil Neville loves Celine Dion and always says her music changed his life. When we were travelling around Australia in pre-season, he was listening to her music all the time."
Mikel Arteta

"Liverpool is such a beautiful city, with a lot of culture – and I love living here. I have even learned how to cook spaghetti and fried eggs."
Li Wei Feng

"I have been living for two-and-a-half weeks in a rented apartment, but here I have nothing. I was told that robbers come for all kinds of clocks and ornaments, but I don't have any. I heard that robbers come and demand that the owner opens his safe. I have one, but I don't use it. I don't even know how to open it."

Diniyar Bilyaletdinov warns off the local burglars

"When I said morning men I thought the women would of [sic] been busy preparing breakfast/getting kids ready/making the beds – sorry women!"

An old Phil Neville tweet he was forced to apologise for

"When I said I had no regrets, I'd forgotten about that haircut and it has come back to haunt me on several occasions."

Trevor Steven on his mullet

"I can drink like a chimney."

Duncan Ferguson

Romelu Lukaku tweets: "Just had some kids doing trick or treat at my door. It's the first time it happened in my life, haha."

FIFA tweets: "What did you do Rom?!"

Lukaku: "Gave them Kit Kats."

An odd Twitter exchange between the striker and FIFA over Hallowe'en

THE FUNNIEST EVERTON QUOTES... EVER!

MANAGING JUST FINE

"That's a home win and an away draw inside four days. We've only got one more game in November and, if we win that, I'm in grave danger of becoming Manager of the Month."
Mike Walker days before he was given the boot

"Today's been a good day for Wayne, but he's understood that on another day it could've been a bad day."
David Moyes

"Phenomenal."
Roberto Martinez on everything!

"Whoever put out the statement saying eight weeks is getting a b*llocking."

Sam Allardyce is angry after he feels Everton's social media team exaggerated Gylfi Sigurdsson's time on the sidelines

"It's not that he doesn't like the press. It's just that he doesn't like talking to them."

Joe Royle on Duncan Ferguson refusing to speak to the media

"If I tell you we will fight for the title, I think most people will tell you that man is crazy."

Ronald Koeman

Q: "What's your impressions of Africa?"

Gordon Lee: "Africa? We're not in bloody Africa, are we?"

The manager speaking in Morocco

"Sorry about the dream final lads. And that's bollocks with a double L!"

Joe Royle after Everton beat Tottenham in the 1995 FA Cup semi which denied the media a Man United v Spurs showpiece

"Philippe [Senderos] was as good as we were going to get in our situation."

David Moyes is underwhelmed by his new loan signing

"He is very happy. I would blame the photographer because it is their job to make him produce a nice smile!... I will chase the photographer because I wasn't happy with that at all!"

Roberto Martinez jokingly blames the snapper for not making Aaron Lennon smile during his Everton unveiling

"Should they give Fergie the England job? Of course. Give the rest of us a bloomin' chance."

Joe Royle

"I'll get you into the Champions League."

What Roberto Martinez apparently told Bill Kenwright

"How do I view Manchester United? Preferably on television. But unfortunately we have to go down the East Lancs Road to get a bit closer."

Howard Kendall

"The first word begins with 'f', the second with 'o'."

David Moyes when asked what his response was to a request for Wayne Rooney to be released for an England U20s away game

"Even when you're dead, you shouldn't let yourself lie down and be buried."

Gordon Lee

"I've never been able to get my hands fully around the top teams and grab them and grasp them and pull them back into us, but there have been times when I've touched them."
David Moyes

"A player must sleep for eight hours, and if I can prove that he has not slept for eight hours, he will get a fine."
Roberto Martinez sleepwalking Everton down the table

"I'm like a dog with two dicks."
Joe Royle after a victory at Chelsea

"We planned to get off to a good start during our pre-season tour to Dallas. The Grassy Knoll was fabulous and nearly all the lads have got theories on who killed JFK."

David Moyes

"He'll be doing the team talk tomorrow. I think he is looking forward to it."

Sam Allardyce jokes Theo Walcott will brief the side ahead of his return to Arsenal

"Some names are true, some are not true. Most of the time it's bullsh*t!"

Ronald Koeman is frank about Everton's reported transfer targets

"We don't have reporters any more – we have QCs. Nowadays they aren't interested in how many goals a player scores, but where he's scoring at night."

Joe Royle

Q: "Is it true you're a fan of the 'Money can't buy you Stones' chant?"

A: "Not really, no. Unless you've been in my house and in my shower!"

Roberto Martinez

"When I came down [from Scotland] everybody told me Everton were a top-six side."

Walter Smith

"If my two league games against Liverpool this season had been a Champions League tie, we'd have gone through. That's something my critics won't tell you."

Sam Allardyce. OK, then!

"Our draws have been more like victories without goals."

Roberto Martinez

Journalist: "Brian Clough has called you 'a young pup'. Do you want to respond?"

Howard Kendall: "I can't. I'm a hush puppy!"

Everton had thumped Clough's side 5-0

"When I called my midfield the 'Dogs of War' it was done half-jokingly. But the game has changed. The playmaker who stands on the ball and sprays it everywhere after five pints and a cigar in the pub simply doesn't exist any more."

Joe Royle

"I want people to look back and say it was a golden period; to create a legacy. We've built slowly and there will be a moment in time soon when we win something. We're getting much closer to doing it."

David Moyes after eight years at the helm... and fans still await a trophy

"At least I'll be able to sleep tonight."

Howard Kendall after a victory over Southampton. It ended up being his final match in charge

"We're going to make sure everybody has to have haggis and porridge in the canteen from now on."

Walter Smith on the high number of Scots at Goodison Park

"The plan is to get out of management while I've still got all my marbles and my hair."

Joe Royle

"As a manager you need to run a football club as if you are going to be here for 100 years."
Roberto Martinez. Erm?

"If Mickey Mouse had taken charge, it would have given the place a lift."
Mike Walker on the state of Everton in 1994

"Everybody used to get him mixed up with Lee Carsley, so when Real Madrid came in for him at Everton, we were saying, 'Have they got the right one? Is Carsley the one or is it Tommy Gravesen?' The two baldies and whatnot."
David Moyes on Thomas Gravesen

"People keep on about stars and flair. For me, you find stars in the sky and flair at the bottom of your trousers."

Gordon Lee

"Towards the end, when he wasn't well, he said to me, 'Everton won't pay me off. They're waiting for me to die'. It's a hard business is football."

Howard Kendall on Harry Catterick

"I have mellowed over the years, I think. I am not sure that is a good thing. Maybe it would be better if I was still a baddy."

David Moyes

"Don't ask me how many marks I'd get out of 10, either... P*ss off. 11!"

Sam Allardyce after a club survey asked fans to score him on a scale of zero to 10

"The transfer request was something he didn't mean to do."

Roberto Martinez on John Stones looking to leave the Toffees

"Any personal insult, be it funny or really personal, does not interest me."

David Unsworth after Joey Barton said: "He's a glorified PE teacher who shouldn't be in charge of a men's team."

"His track record has got no comparison what-soever with mine. He got Hull City relegated."
Sam Allardyce on then-Watford manager Marco Silva – before being replaced by him

"You quickened your pace when you saw him. I spent six years as his captain but couldn't tell you what he was like as a bloke. The people he employed, his coaching staff, didn't like him. We players were terrified of him. His great skill was identifying players and balancing his team."
Howard Kendall on his old manager Harry Catterick

"There are very few journalists now, just a lot of quote collectors and back-stabbers; hitmen waiting for something to happen."

Joe Royle falls out with some of the press

"I don't do the internet so I only hear about [the rumours] when you people tell me."

Technophobe David Moyes dismisses speculation about his future

"I soon got out of the habit of studying the top end of the league table."

Walter Smith on how managing Everton differs with Rangers

BOARDROOM BANTER

"My mum rang up when she heard I wanted to take over the club and said, 'Oh son, don't'. Only an 11-year-old boy would want to get into something like this."

Bill Kenwright

"I think David Moyes is the greatest manager in the world bar none and he's my best friend in football and I'd do anything for him."

Kenwright is madly in love

"He uttered the six worst words in the English language: 'I want to play for Liverpool'."

Kenwright on Nick Barmby's Reds move

"You'd think we'd brought Desperate Dan and Corky the Cat in."

The chairman reacts to critics of the club's stadium plans

"Are you trying to tell me there's a bigger club than Everton? Do me a favour. Wayne Rooney is going nowhere."

When Kenwright was asked if Rooney would end up joining "a bigger club". The player left inside the year

"Football is a bitch goddess."

Not sure what the Everton chief means?

TALKING BALLS

"He's a Spaniard, who has come from Spain."

Phil Neville on Mikel Arteta

"Andy Gray is an ugly b*stard in the morning and I can vouch for that because I've slept with him a few times."

John Bailey

"Wayne Rooney can go all the way to the top if he keeps his head firmly on the ground."

David Unsworth

"He had a first touch like a tackle."

Neville Southall on Brett Angel

"I know Duncan Ferguson is Scottish but deep down he's a Scouser – he's more Scouse than half the people I know around here."

Tony Hibbert

"I was the best in black and white and Nev was the best in colour."

Gordon West on Neville Southall

"When Andy Gray came to Everton, I told him he was my favourite player when I was a young boy. And he said, 'Sod off, you cheeky monkey, how old do you think I am?'"

Graeme Sharp

"He had a way of looking at people that frightened them, but I shared rooms with him for a considerable number of years and he was a pussycat."

Gary Stevens on Pat Van Den Hauwe

"£5m for a centre-half who can't head the ball!"

Leon Osman on Per Kroldrup

"The good thing about Nev was that he didn't drink, so when we roomed together he used to wake up early and make me a cup of tea."

Alan Harper on Neville Southall

"Well done lad, but remember, you're still only half as good as I was."

Dixie Dean to Bob Latchford after his 30th league goal

[Bobby Gould] would make a great double glazing salesman. We had a meeting and by the end we were all thinking, 'When's he going to sell us a new car?'"

Neville Southall

"Mick Lyons thought he was playing for England in every game, even in training."

Kevin Ratcliffe

Duncan Ferguson: "By the way, have you clocked the new physio? It's Bob the f*cking Builder. I'm Big Dunc, I've finished a few f*cking physios' careers."

Physio Mick Rathbone: "I'm Baz, I've finished a few players' careers."

Ferguson: "F*cking brilliant. I'm gonna like you."

Rathbone: "Well it's just as well because you spend the season in the medical room, don't you?"

"What can I say about him? Where do you want me to start? He's the softest lad I've met in a long time."

Neville Southall on Duncan Ferguson

"He had this crazy Danish-Scouse accent. Once he brought a paintball gun in and just started just shooting people."

James McFadden on Thomas Gravesen

"He was Moyes' pet so I picked on him a lot. I think he told everything that was going on to the boss and that's why he was captain, he was a snitch."

Andy van der Meyde on Phil Neville

"Jesus Christ, Durranty. What the f*ck are you doing here? Do you realise the state we're in?"

Paul Rideout to ex-teammate Ian Durrant, who arrived on loan from Rangers

PUNDIT PARADISE

"David Moyes does like to get dirty with his players."
Charlie Nicholas

"If Everton got any deeper, they'd be in Stanley Park."
Jamie Carragher gives his verdict on Everton's tactics

"Everton, they've got Cahill, Osman and Pienaar. They're not household names – maybe not even in their own houses."
Eamon Dunphy watching Everton against Arsenal

"I cover Everton matches too. But if war was declared, I think I know which side I'd be on."

Ex-Liverpool star, now pundit, Tommy Smith

"It's now much more 50-50 in favour of Everton."

Iain Dowie

"It's good to have your full-backs coming forward, like Gary Neville does here for Everton."

Lee Dixon mixes up his Nevilles in Everton's clash with Aston Villa

"Everton really are a bag of Revels."

Paul Merson

"If you don't give him a chance, what chance has he got?"

Paul Merson on the chances of Roberto Martinez finding those early wins

"Keep your mouth shut, do your job, go home, have your tea and play football."

Phil Neville's advice to Loris Karius after the Liverpool goalie had a war of words with his brother Gary

"Everton have not won without being in the lead."

Andy Gray during the Merseyside derby

"It was the game that pu[t] on the road."

Alan Green

"It's Arsenal 0, Everton 1. And the longer it stays like that the more you've got to fancy Everton to win."

John Motson

"Two-and-a-half minutes that cat was on the pitch and they couldn't get him. He did more running than some of the Everton players apparently... but that's a bit unfair."

Gary Lineker after a feline went onto the field during Everton's defeat to Wolves

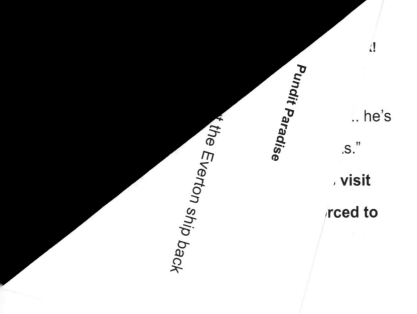

Pundit Paradise

the Everton ship back

.! he's .s."

visit rced to

"I'm definitely go... weather was incredible – it was like Miami. And yes, I'm an Everton fan now."

Stallone on his Merseyside trip in 2007

"When Everton knock it long, they don't knock it long."

Paul Merson

"Marouane Fellaini is suspended for today's match, so he is sitting in the stand watching today's game. I'd hate to be the poor sod behind him, though."

Unknown journalist writing BBC's Live Text for Everton's clash with Liverpool

"I've seen worse. But not very often."

Johnny Giles is enjoying Everton's match against Birmingham

"Merseyside derbies usually last 90 minutes and I'm sure today's won't be any different."

Trevor Brooking

"The Everton fans are massed in the Station End, and Lee Carsley is attacking those fans now."

John Murray

"Fellaini has put a spanner in the wheels."

Bobby Gould

Printed in Great Britain
by Amazon